NEAR MISS

NEAR MISS

LAURA MATWICHUK

NIGHTWOOD EDITIONS

2019

Nightwood Editions
P.O. Box 1779
Gibsons, BC, V0N 1V0, Canada
www.nightwoodeditions.com

EDITOR: Amber McMillan
COVER DESIGN & TYPOGRAPHY: Carleton Wilson
COVER ART: Ryan Peter, *Untitled (Autogram)*, 2013

Canada

Nightwood Editions acknowledges the support of the Canada Council for the Arts, which last year invested $153 million to bring the arts to Canadians throughout the country.

Nous remercions le Conseil des arts du Canada de son soutien. L'an dernier, le Conseil a investi 153 millions de dollars pour mettre de l'art dans la vie des Canadiennes et des Canadiens de tout le pays.

We also gratefully acknowledge financial support from the Government of Canada and from the Province of British Columbia through the BC Arts Council and the Book Publishing Tax Credit.

This book has been produced on 100% post-consumer recycled, ancient-forest-free paper, processed chlorine-free and printed with vegetable-based dyes.

Printed and bound in Canada.

LIBRARY AND ARCHIVES CANADA CATALOGUING IN PUBLICATION

Matwichuk, Laura, author
Near miss / Laura Matwichuk.

Poems.
Issued in print and electronic formats.
ISBN 978-0-88971-353-6 (softcover).--ISBN 978-0-88971-141-9 (ebook)

I. Title.

PS8626.A8826N43 2019   C811'.6   C2018-904792-5
                                            C2018-904793-3

for JB and BB

CONTENTS

INFERNO

And we would go on as though nothing was wrong.
– Joy Division

1700   Cascadia megathrust   Geriatric evergreens shiver
                    through morning water aerobics
          under a domed sky of pastel rose,   glinting copper.
                              Are you alive?

1946   Vancouver Island swings open like a broken hinge,
                    birthing a rock slide of cranky descendants.
          I didn't expect the smoke from these fires to reach you.
                              Are you safe?

1949   Bedrock-mounted seismometers fumble,
                    etch secret messages from Haida Gwaii
                        on photographic paper.
          Did you see me,   sailing a crooked boat
                        across the sea?

1970   Fault creep,   buildup,   geometric irregularities.
                    I cannot adhere my body to any surface.
          Ground spins asymmetrical,
                    thermostats explode with paranoia
                        but life isn't ruined.

2012   The sea salivates bad feelings,
                    horizontal strain,
                        unbearable lithosphere load.
          I don't care.
                    Worrying about the end has aged me.
          It's been three hundred and seventeen years since we last spoke.

INSOMNIA

DECOMMISSIONED PLANES

It's not easy to pull the track blinds,
look for cedar waxwings or passenger
jets through Dad's cheapo binoculars,
check the furnace filters, pilot light,
as engines rumble overhead.
Decommissioned planes in long-term
storage in the Mojave are obsolete
yet invincible. Because of the dry climate,
they don't rust, parts are recycled
or sold to foreign nations to keep
other planes in the air. You examine
aerial photographs, satellite images,
painterly trails of hydraulic fluid soaking
into sand. When the Emergency Broadcast
System proclaims *This is only a test*, you
leave the TV on because you've gotten
used to the sound. You keep waiting
for the heat to come on, for the regular
broadcast to resume, for a new sensation
to quicken inside you like the sight
of that fleet of ghost-planes lifted
from the desert, reanimated, hovering
over your house like everything is fine.

STRANGE MIGRATION

A girl in a pedestrian underpass covers one eye, says: *Home is no place*. She has an idea of what life could be. Her shoulders slope away like eastern rivers. She suspects the strange migration of the alpacas is a consequence of the weather. These ones, here, are getting heat stroke. She transports a secret herd by boxcar, hidden behind a mountain of splintered crates, muffled by chicken songs. At night she records the distant cries of the alpha males with a portable microphone, their fur falling off in the snow. Double-crested cormorants sleep more often than she does. Drinking a root beer, she thinks of sleepovers cut short, back home around Dad's shoulders in a nightgown and boots. How he taught her three ways to feel better. One was: *Go watch TV*.

What's gotten into you?

DAUGHTERS

There are pirate daughters in the substation
sealing leaks with chewing gum. Daughters
are waiting for congressional committees
to break for lunch. It's the quarter-birthday
of this daughter, who is going to build
a great building. One daughter has a few
questions about where this hatchback
is taking her. Daughters are becoming members.
Daughters are meeting sons behind parochial
schools, feet dropping like bricks into Friday-
night hot tubs. Daughters are attending
rehearsals, perfecting their Olgas, Marias,
Irinas. Daughters might even sleep tonight,
but have stopped dreaming of underwater
back flips and sandlot sirs. Daughters are trying
to stop saying *ummmm*. Daughters are tuning out
the voices of their mothers: *Is that blackbird
your daughter or mine? Your daughter did **what**
to my daughter's science experiment?* Daughters
are meeting on tarpaper roofs to braid typewriter
ribbons, eight-track cartridges and reel-to-reels.
Daughters are tethering kites to the suburbs,
cooing into tunnels of no return.

Mid-air,
passengers speak out.

Collision-warning system   closing in.

Window,

white airplane,

     our airplane.

Woosh   underneath.

Parallel sky.

"It was going to hit us."

     JetBlue   airspace.

Close calls over Long Island, JFK,

         Newark.

SMOKE DETECTOR

When the karate students commence
knife-hand strikes to the neck

in their too-bright studio, I head for home.
Neon orange *Rented!* tags are hooked

on empty clamshells of new releases
in the darkened window of the video store.

Cardboard box behind the locked door
overflowing with late returns reminds me:

people are just trying to be good. It's not
our fault we live in Tudor-revival houses,

pastel gauze curtains framing our nocturnal
activities—it isn't supposed to be sad.

The quarry visible from our cul-de-sac
at night has a fence lassoed tight around it—

for everyone's protection—glowing yellow
of the limestone mountain, a category

of temptation no one foresaw. I may never
know who trimmed the innermost tree

on the freeway median into the shape
of a giant almond, or how a photograph

of it ended up on our fridge door, or why
it remained there for more than a decade

under a magnet in the shape of a rose.
As I lift the pitcher of ice water from the shelf,

I'm reminded there's no great mystery
to solid objects, yet they're powerful enough

to change the way I feel. After the drought,
Dad will soak the lawn with a sprinkler

and Mom will wave a towel beneath the smoke
detector. At midnight, my public library fines

will begin to carry greater value than the paper-
backs to which they were assigned.

The rolling blackout dream. The melted cassette lying in a hedge dream. The buying a Himalayan salt lamp from the health food store and getting my hopes up as I walk home dream. The too many sports metaphors dream. The watching the track-meet medal ceremony from a distance dream. The broken escalator dream. The I'm not crying, I just have something in my eye dream. The I'm not crying, I just have really bad hay fever dream. The I'm not crying, I've just been staring at a computer screen which gives me dry eyes dream. The recurring dream in which you fall down carpeted stairs and feel exhausted. The finding out there's no such thing as a hand-held device to predict earthquakes dream. The fragmented audio recording which sounds less and less like a human voice over time dream. The awkward visit to the famous sculptor's studio dream. The dream in which an incriminating answering machine message is played before a full auditorium of detectives. The writing algebraic equations on the chalkboard until it is full right up to the edges and contains everything you know dream. The dream in which you say prime numbers mean nothing to me to an old woman in a swimming pool and she floats away on her back. The dream in which you tell a fellow graduate student you've read Of Grammatology, but you've really only seen a documentary about Derrida buttering a piece of toast. The watching Joe Versus the Volcano and feeling like maybe you have a brain cloud too dream. The lying awake at night because anthrax is leaking out of glacial ice dream. The dream of translucent walls that keep expanding. The dream of liquid becoming gas.

PROXIMITY SENSORS

Theremin practice commences at six o'clock, tonal quiver accompanying playoff recaps, five-day forecasts, bleak dispatches from the war zone. To better hear the voice of a reporter on the ground in Grozny, Mom clicks the volume up two notches. Removes her glasses, breathes on each lens, wipes. An eight-foot privacy fence and mature hedge of western red cedar surround our yard. Sound barrier of sculpted branches. When the upright antenna's vertical limit is reached, I make micro-adjustments to amplitude, frequency. During commercial breaks, eerie sounds compete with revolutions in dish soap, ergonomic toothbrush technology. Leaf blower with four-stroke engine guaranteed to change the way you think about autumn. Mom never says a word, but when an investigative report on a surge in violent crime across the boroughs prompts another three clicks on the remote, I lower my arms as if to say *I feel you*. The result of a Russian-government-sponsored research project, the Theremin was originally designed to "detect nearby objects without physical contact." Only later was its spooky musical potential realized. Outside, the sky is blurting out dusk and Dad's up a ladder, calmly replacing the bulbs in motion floodlights near the eaves. Little spies, they operate by involuntary reflex, safeguarding the dark zone between garage and gate. Steadfast at detecting prowling cats, they have never, to my knowledge, fallen on the shoulders of an intruder.

CARTOGRAPHY

This map says our coal is going to Japan.
It summarizes knowledge circa 1982,
arranges chunks of carbon at my feet
without any need for explanation.
Blackened layers of peat, a river of rags—
these are the map's concerns. At seven
years old, I don't know what to do
with this information. There's "enormous
potential in hydro-electricity, wood waste,
natural gas." I lose concentration
for a moment as elders push chairs back
above my head. Insulation, wood,
linoleum, I work my way up to the soles
of their feet under the kitchen table.
"Non-conventional energy sources include
wind, solar, geothermal and small hydro."
The Okanagan is lousy with uranium
deposits. Now I know. Affixed to the rec-
room wall with two gold push pins,
the bottom corners curl. In the window
well, a brief parade of ankles flutter by,
changing the light. Glaciers and ice fields
are pistachio, then kelly green. "Average
monthly wave power off Tofino is 35.1 kW/m
of crest." Just because a value is assigned
doesn't mean it will last. A gravity-packed
unit is a measurement for hog fuel, which
isn't what it sounds like. There are coal
fields in Merritt. No one told me.
Wind is virtually everywhere, that much

I figured out on my own. I won't request
a copy of this map from the Ministry of Energy,
but it has taught me something about
the direction we're headed, the suddenly
shifting energy of what we know.

Swarm unseen   in US skies.
*   Quadcopter drone,*
*   restricted airspace.*
Silver altitude   too close to airports.
*   Previously undisclosed fits surge.*

When close calls pose a
*   headache,*
*   decline, intercept,*
*   soar over the tidal basin.*

January lockdown,
Strike Eagle,
*   Goshawk near Yuma, Ariz.,*
buzzed, robotic.
*   Coloured lights of John F. Kennedy in nature.*

"The number of near misses is

astounding."

A sensitive satellite.

Vast,
safe,
real.

INSOMNIA

The buzz of midnight mowing prevents sleep, but this isn't the only issue. The bedside clock is new, but old-timey, with an inoperable bell and little hammers. Setting the alarm begins the process. As my doctor suggested, I make reasonable goals for the hours ahead: visualize the skateboard park, figure-eight loops through a bathtub of graffiti. Tomorrow I might hum murder ballads into a tin can. But when the TV fills with snow, chances are I will be sitting here, reading the dictionary: "Frontier: a part of a country that borders on another country." (A pang of guilt: on Tuesday we burgled the neighbours' tool shed, made a bet they would never miss the trowel. You called it harmless, moving the record player needle to the edge.) Are those Russian overtures on the portable radio, or the small bells of your keychain through the fog? I can't tell. I unpacked boxes with my mother after the divorce. She kept my fourth-grade math assignments, called the penmanship "top-notch." It is this sort of thing that keeps me up at night.

Dream of small fires,
hazy nebulae. Saltwater
sloshing in a shoreward boat.
Smiling gold-dust sky. Mountain
imprint gone, and with it, all sense of
north. Slurred basins of neon algal blooms
harbouring colonies of mosquitoes.
Fir trees tall as cellphone towers.
Cellphone towers tall as redwoods.
Indoor fountains dyed turquoise
with underwater lights.
Bath of blue pine cones,
a mouth that opens.

SEISMOPHOBIA

Splits you in half,
morphs into hard chunks
behind your sternum.
Pains like the cracking
away of a trillion-ton iceberg
from Antarctica's ghostly
skeleton. You cling
to the temporary relief
of dusk, gradual collapse
of Pacific-coastline
details. To errant sparks
from small fires, shimmying
over a silhouetted peak,
quick as bloodthirsty insects.
To the dumb sound
of crumpled beer cans
clinking against rock,
compensating for silence
everywhere else. Whatever
techniques failed you
once are worth a second try.
When you've surrendered
to the worst your brain
can conjure, the dark
will make it up to you,
diurnal tides will carry you,
your body will be
phosphorescent light.

WINTER DIVE

Late December mornings on the diving board, red-throated loons drawing circles in the chlorinated water, fat shadows against tile. Every three minutes or so, the air clouds with steam from a little wooden hut nearby. Occupants emerge, ruby-faced, to drop towels and lumber into the shallow end. Shall I forfeit, or will I need a nudge? The shot of a pistol or prick of a pirate's blade might coax me to the edge, but let's be realistic: I will never salvage coins, dive deep for neon tackle. In the locker room, I overheard two unshaven women say you can buy cold tea in a glass for a dollar near the tennis courts, but a cuckold with a gym bag is waiting in the parking lot and paper snowflakes are peeling away from the windows.

What have you been told?

PRIZE RIBBONS

Stealing prize ribbons from the fairground,
you award yourself third for grooming;
best in show for me, the suggestion alone
too much to live up to. Above our heads,
a thin wire dotted with acrylic marking balls:
bright orange globes rated first in weather-
ability and visible from a great distance,
even at night. Slowly, I'm getting used to them.
If you're the gleaming wings of a cargo jet,
I'm the rickety wheels a prop-plane tucks
into itself after takeoff that cause the pilot's brow
to furrow for the rest of the flight. Crossing
a field ringed with gravel, dusted with leaves,
I act like winning isn't everything, remain
focused on low-lying patterns even as the big
picture eludes me. Accidentally-on-purpose
toss my ribbon to the wind above the bike
racks. If you haven't noticed by now, I care
deeply who dies first and who gets left here,
stuck in an eternal lap. Hate not knowing.
At dusk, unremarkable floodlights click
on to help us see the way forward. A small
glider touches down on the flat grass oval
and all the sweaty runners stand still.

INTERIOR MYSTERIES

Piano movers idle on the corner
with a pair of walnut uprights,
lower an aluminum ramp onto the driveway.
Prodigies convene in a private green
room before the competition, size
each other up. With wool blazers
bunching in armpits and towers
of metronomes twitching, their hands
and brains stay synchronized.

I think I've seen what they call
topography: vast planes contoured
with bluish hypsometric tints,
lacquered hardwood shrinking
and swelling. But surfaces don't interest
me much. I prefer the hidden
landscape of felt and wire beneath
the soundboard's thick inches.

In 2007, a Bösendorfer 275 purchased
for forty-five thousand pounds at auction
fell thirteen feet from the back of a truck
onto a grass embankment in Devon,
England, revealing its Austrian spruce
bones to the sky. *It's the worst thing
that's ever happened to me,* the mover said.
Deemed repairable by experts, the instrument's
interior mysteries remained a caveat
to their diagnosis: some effects,
they warned, take years to materialize.

Acid rain drips from black holes in the library ceiling.

You gather cellophaned hardcovers, laminated softcovers and musty
    bound journals.

You've seen all the wooden chairs filled up with bodies and emptied again.

Seen the moon shape-shift through diamonds of leaded glass.

You are reading a boring article about squalls when the power cuts.

Outside, a sloppy flag strangles its pole.

Three-ring binder releases a quilt of loose-leaf into a fountain.

Now you're a sensitive instrument, counting acorns, sleepwalking
    through hedges.

You are a bucket gently lifting a torn wire back to its place among the trees.

SUBALPINE WONDERS

A smile from the past can be terrifying. Inherited genetic character-istics say *Boo!* then grab your ankles. In the photograph from '68, my teenaged mother stands with her sisters at the edge of Lake Louise, a hotel looming like bad weather above their windswept hair. Who can say how they coped?

I shouldn't have come. Summer demotes the glacier to pure liquid in an endless repetition, yet the photo can never be replicated: a thin woman bending over wiry stems of pink and orange poppies. Tan teenagers in shirt sleeves playing a game on the lawn.

If there's a trace of my mother buried in the Shoreline Trail gravel—her latent shoeprint, a corner of her heel—it's long expired, as impossible to lift from the water's margin as from our last phone conversation. By now, I should know better, keep expectations low.

Like the proverbial hook dropping into the ice-fishing hole, the tem-perature will plummet soon. Victoria Glacier will creak and shine. The chateau, once enormous, will shrink into darkness, even as its mass endures.

Life isn't like that. From what I've seen, it can't withstand even the slightest pressure. Mom tried to make up for it, though, in her way. Once, in the eighties, she filled an inflatable pool with a garden hose, convinced me it was a lake.

AFTER YOUR FUNERAL

Hearing aid feedback fills the church sanctuary.
Panicked, I escape through miles of muskeg, black spruce
and jack pine. Abandoned brickyards and nickel mines.

Past ravens perched in a contented ring formation
around an anodyne pond, charcoal throats neatly
smocked with down. Banded elms along the boulevards
will be unwrapped in early June, cankerworms

staved off for another season. I struggle to remain
upright on the sidewalk with all this death hanging
around. The architect who choked in Pennsylvania

Station? His Salk Institute will stand forever.
While scientists map the human genome, water flows
through the courtyard of La Jolla, near the roots
of dying lime trees. I will bring their good news

to your gravestone. An hour with the chalk-browed
mockingbirds feels more than enough, I've had my fill
of their wheezy repertoire, dull brown plumage.

The Manitoba Wildlife Centre offers protection
across four cardinal points. At the corner of Portage
and Main, beleaguered window-washers scale bank
towers with Bosun's chair and bucket, ropes attached

to scaffolds out of view. A little death reflected back
in each squeegeed pane. I read medical journals
for my job, which might be worse. Based on the abstracts
you'd think cancer was just frenetic multiplication,

twirling strands of DNA. Scientists admit that after
billions of dollars in research, they remain in the dark
about most aspects of the disease. Soap in their eyes,
they swing for landings they cannot see.

FUJI, BABY

As the HR MacMillan Space Centre's
sky theatre goes dim, my thoughts flip
back like a page to Honshu Island,

tourists ascending eroded, trash-laden
paths under cover of darkness to glimpse
milky morning light from Fuji's summit.

Recently, I watched a video of the sun
rising to calm myself. Then clicked on
a weird time-lapse GIF depicting how

a mother's internal organs move out
of the way as her baby grows. When I tried
to find it again to show you, I couldn't

get the search term right. I can't forget
how the sonographer paused, trans-
ducer in hand, to say, *Let's double-check*

that, her words a fault line in my heart
cracking open. After the appointment,
I took a taxi to meet you for the concert,

frantically Googling "normal bi-parietal
diameter" en route, too petrified to read
the results generated. You said the musician

was hosting a workshop, Laugh with Laraaji,
to help people get in touch with their inner
children. I couldn't tell if you were confessing

a desire to attend, mentioning it for my sake,
or as a joke. Sure, I've been under some stress
lately. Moving slow as a parade float

drenched in tinsel. Because my heart hurts.
Doubled blood volume roiling like lava
through four red chambers. Each day, up

with the sunrise because my inner child
is a metaphor and a literal tiny child kicking
me awake. Myself and someone else,

two me's. When he flipped into breach,
I spent a week doing inversions on the carpet.
You shone an incandescent flashlight

at my belly, placed foam headphones
around it. On the advice of the acupuncturist,
burned moxa by my pinkie toes, hoping

the heat would transmit a message
to our son: go easy on me. Everyone in the sky
theatre is twenty-three and high, not

pregnant. They smell like sweat and spear-
mint gum. I don't care anymore. Laraaji
is banging a gong and cackling

into a microphone as galaxies slide on curved
screens above his head. He wears robes
the colour of the scorching sun. Sometimes

laughter swims through the body like a sound
wave travelling back to the probe as an echo
but there's no GIF depicting this. Cherry

blossoms fall like floral meteors into a pond
behind the planetarium at the same rate
of speed as at the base of Fuji. A mother

eagle assembles a sturdy moss-and-feather
loft for her newborns in the highest tree
in Vanier Park because the view is nice.

Perhaps Japanese bird mothers do the same,
because who wouldn't want the very best
for their children's eyeballs? Who

wouldn't want to listen to the calming
sounds of Laraaji's collaborator Brian Eno
during thirty-nine hours of labour

followed by emergency C-section?
You place an iPod beside the hospital
bathtub and Apollo drowns out my screams.

I see stars. Fly to Japan. Leave Earth's
atmosphere in a nitrous-fuelled rocket ship.
Beta blockers slow pyroclastic flows

in my heart through the worst of it. Even
in this altered state, I'm only pretending
I don't know what is happening to me.

I know. As they lift the tiny person over
the paper scaffolding and place him
on my chest like a warm island, the sun rises

over a mountain of ash and snow, carving
living pathways through the maternity ward.

SHADOW PUPPETS

We don't have time for this, Mom says. *Dump your souvenirs in the backseat, wave goodbye to your cousins.* But my eyes are too full, I'm a grain silo. I see a deep black crater in the football field behind her, spire of the community church burning on the horizon.

The circular sneeze we share around the dinner table functions as a kind of prayer, and when she boils the potatoes everyone pitches in, rubbing clear spots on the windows with shirtsleeves, turning chairs upside down, seat to tabletop. Not me though, because there it is again. Ring of bright flame in plain view beside the garage: a neighbour's bungalow obliterated.

Another word for crater is "depression." A possible cause for depression is "internal collapse." Sneak out the patio door, and just when I think proof's within reach, the fiery glow fades forever. What's left to depend on when the mind plays tricks? Mom doesn't answer, instead sculpts three shadow puppets on my bedroom wall: pyramids of Giza, space station orbiting the earth, herd of bison walking a perfect line across the prairie.

When was the last time you slept?

INTERIOR

HERE COMES THE FUTURE

It always looks darkest just before it gets totally black.
– Charlie Brown

We name the barn swallows Nemo and Nova.
They build a nest in our binoculars:
pellets of mud, moth wings, horsehair.

I lean over the developer baths.
Through the chemical sheen, a grainy shape
slides toward a fissure in the ice.

Maybe that's Alaska.

Sandbags twist on ropes while I read books
about Scotch-broom sneezes, cough-syrup
moustaches, trampoline bounces
and water balloons.

Volunteers shuffle through the security gate,
set their hands on hips to make decisions.

Retching sounds fill the concrete parkade,
but I wait for you.

Last week you taught me how to brush my teeth
in the river with a little cup.

After dinner, I pretend to start a fire
and you sprinkle nails in the drive.

With mittened hands, we push most of the snow
from the door, slip-crawl under fence wires
to reconnect torn cables.

For a while, I devote myself to Etch-a-Sketch
renderings of pale nightjars in the yard,
spindly winter-peeled trees.

You spin bouquets of tobacco, oxblood
blossoms. I read books about kaleidoscopes
and wiffle balls.

Wood smoke leaks a dove-grey trail
across the bedroom. Time maps our foreheads.
The news anchor does preparatory
throat exercises on the little TV.

Dear lover of the mid-aughts,
of years crowded with wisecracks and tears:
I am keeping your temperature
with me. In dreams, lake water slides
through my inner ear and cicadas awaken.

Sometimes I fill our pillowcases
with lucky ticker tape salvaged from
the astronaut's return to earth.

In the lobby of the Vladivostok Museum,
I swallow multivitamins and read books
about magicians and grocery lists,
cult films and carpool lanes.

There's a new ghost at the circulation
kiosk, but she's friendly.

Mom said your hand would come loose
from mine like a wishbone snapping.

I build a moon rock diorama to scale
in the garage. A tin of brittle sand dollars
freezes on the window ledge.
The blender's kaput.

We spill our drinks in the room you named
parlour. I count ten dormer windows
under the red dwarf. Read books about dry-erase
boards and parkas, dowagers and bat wings.

Whitecap tantrums peter out, shed salt
ribbons on the shore.

We cross the ice field in pursuit of tranquilizers.
All we need is something hard and artificial.
Blue schools in the estuary

slide like ink through a new tattoo.

A cotton sheet saves a few of the starlings.
The rest go to sleep under ombré popsicle sticks.

I read books about alarm codes,
confectioners' sugar, nightshade, curses.

In marriage costumes, we paddle
across the Lite-Brite sea.

You say our children will be born
under that metal braid of power lines.
It's the only time we speak about imaginary things.
I pin eyelashes to the cork-board memorial,
fill trash bags with raspberries.
What was it we used to do for fun?

Didn't grow up in a factory town,
but we loitered in catwalks where time
was lazy, where hedges thickened slow,
curled through wire diamonds.

Now I drag fallen twigs along this surface,
catching on the holes.

Can't remember Petri dish experiments
or litmus tests, but I do keep
a stethoscope in the bed beside me.

When a storm takes the siding, our neighbours
lean the vinyl pieces in their garage
until we come by.

You seem to know exactly where to put pressure
on a secret to break it.

I read books about Kodiaks and salmon,
plums and cancer.

I unzip your mascot head in the car
by the duck pond. We fly north in the morning
so you can teach Intro to Something.

While packing, I find envelopes of old negatives:
tiny Christmases next to tiny Christmas Eves.

We belong to a book club, but want to get out.

I confess to my therapist about the origin
of a stain on the carpet of my childhood home.

I worry about the privacy of revolving doors,
the crush of Polish flowers, the deepest paper cuts.

I read books about coast guards and badminton,
secret societies and heated floors.

In today's political climate, there's no room
for cinephiles.

In the woods near Chilliwack, a checkpoint
where lights swish in and out of our backpacks.
I lean my head back to find the horizon.
Do it over and over.

I read books about vaccinations and foxes,
lens flares and wrapping paper.

Sometimes I grope around in the dark
for a deer bed, an atlas, a remedy.

Thalassic whirlpools disappear under damask
and bone, walnut and oyster.

Overall, we're coping better than some:
we can still run a few miles
before turning around, can still feel the depth
of the hole once we slip inside.

I read books about pancake landings
and wind shears.

I understand little of what I've read.

Is a nocturne a night song or a song
you write while sleeping?

Am I the deep sea that swells up to the bridge
deck, or the tiny cyclist in rain-proof pants
who stops her spinning?

I've memorized wilderness survival tips,
but get lost in the humour.

I shake cinnamon out of the sailcloth
and look everywhere for our downy twins.

You begin to sing a future in my ear.
I settle down.

INFERNO

You cut ash plumes out of magazines,
        mostly geometric shapes.
Trapezoid plumes, rhombus plumes.
Plumes with the edge of a plane wing still visible.
Geode plumes that keep sparkly secrets.
Eruption column encroaching on the corner of a building.
Water tower enveloped by a dizzying, white, cumulonimbus mass.
You crease the shape, tape the edges.
The paper is real and architectural.
        You feel sad because you've made something beautiful
that is also a shelter to protect you
from you don't know what.

THE REAL THING

Fly to Yellowstone to see for ourselves: cruising altitude, circadian rhythm loss, molecules messed up by time. The historic continuity of Old Faithful calms us. We sleep in electric skies. Dream black and white Ansel Adams photographs. Dream live webcam feeds which automatically refresh every twenty seconds. Once, we stared at a photograph on a museum wall until a docent politely told us to stop. There is an appropriate amount of time to stand in contemplation of art and we'd crossed it. Now it's sunrise at the cone geyser and our shutters will not close. Tourist wanders into the shot, disrupting the vista. Adams' tripod teeters on rock. A photograph surrounded by stanchions begs to be stared at. It's not what it looks like. Our insides are flooded—continuous gallons but no waves. For the first time in years, I recall the thing that happened at the Lake Hotel. Long, low formations of limestone and shale. A tripod steadied by two large boulders. Black "West Thumb" of Yellowstone Lake, Riddle and Delusion in the distance. Empty cup teetering on the seatback tray like a suicidal diver. All this endless repetition and we haven't changed one bit: You still believe the real thing will be better than pixels. I still hope Mr. Fifteen-C will move his neck pillow without my having to ask.

Seeing land near the runway,
we investigate, take action.

The radio tower
a hundred feet below us.

Colour not close enough
to tell.

Head home, passengers.

Congested airspace, so little room
for error in crowded skies.

SOUVENIRS

Glass Christmas ornament from Mount St. Helens.

Decorative egg from Sakurajima.

Bubble-wrapped Krakatoa coffee mug.

Sixteen-ounce Haleakala beer glass.

"I Love Vesuvius" paperweight.

"I Love Cotopaxi" iPhone case.

Mount Nyiragongo bookmark.

Bar of ash soap from Eyjafjallajökull.

Five-hundred-piece puzzle of evening light hitting Chimborazo's
    north side, two alpacas.

Refrigerator magnet from Montserrat's Soufrière Hills.

Hawaii Volcanoes National Park Centennial pin.

Bottled Merapi ash.

Hologram bumper sticker depicting a heart-shaped steam cloud
    above Bulusan.

V-neck El Chichón T-shirt.

Mauna Loa "Wish you were here" notecard set with matching envelopes.

Bezymianny 2016 pocket calendar.

Lava-rock pendant necklace on a sterling silver chain from Rainier.

Carved lava rock ashtray from Mount Pavlof.

Huaynaputina bird feeder.

"I Climbed Lassen" green and orange, iron-on fabric patch.

MEET ME IN LITTLE VENICE

Because your leg is still broken,
we make several unscheduled stops
along the Grand Canal, former site
of nautical spectacles. According
to our brochure, Louis XIV's model
ships once looped the liquid runway
where grotesque fish now slurp algae.

You crouch in discomfort, but there's
no time to linger when each vista
in France's premier tourist attraction
spills into the next, a labyrinth
of seamless gardens. I wish we could
skip Little Venice and be fine with it.
Instead, it's the finish line we limp

toward, catching our quadrupled
reflections in gilt-framed mirrors
lining the marathon route. Pedestrian
traffic flows quickly away from us
in search of guided tours, orange juice
kiosks, La Buvette du Dauphin.
Is that what winning looks like?

Sweaty and injured, we'll never achieve
it. I'm prepared to go the distance,
but as the late October sun manufactures
movement on the surface of the Swiss
Ornamental Lake, you stop. Sun your
withered ankle at the water's edge, Aircast
Walking Boot upright in royal grass.

HOME STRETCH
for J. B.

When ten lanes narrow back to two
somewhere east of the Port Mann
without the slightest tectonic rumble
from the Cascadia Subduction Zone,
we rest a little easier against our seat-
belts, turn up the volume on the radio.
In recent years, we've lost track
of the Gateway expansion timeline,
but who hasn't? Three-billion-dollar
budget, two structures bearing little
resemblance now share a name.
Between gleaming cables taut
as picture-frame wire, I glance
at the pitiful remnants of the old
four-lane deck. Half-dismantled,
it's a floating hazard now, will never
again reach land. As an electronic toll
system monitors our crossing via radio
frequency, I'm reminded we've been
together long enough for such systems
to be invented. Funds withdrawn
like air from our accounts as we sleep.
Deep in the home stretch, but what's
that up ahead? Busted overpass
newly reinforced with three bolts
and a thin metal plate where the semi's
trailer struck. Load-bearing capacity
holds for now, but it's a good reminder

that we can't shut our eyes to the signs.
I have always worried and you have
given me every benefit of the doubt.
Homes sparsely scattered on the valley
hills appear warm and harmless.
Between great white cisterns, they flash
their tiny porch lights at America.

NIGHT VISION

They say no one can adjust
to a twenty-eight-hour day,
not even moles. The more we talk
about them, the less I know.

It's two in the morning, but the light
is early afternoon. Lenticular
clouds red as poppies fill the sky.

A couple of drunks remove
their shoes and socks on the sidewalk.
Newcomers, we are not yet accustomed
to looking away.

We hope hypomania is not contagious.
I buy a sleeping mask, melatonin
from the Medicine Chest Pharmacy.
You place a square of cardboard
in our bedroom window.

At night we lie beside it,
trying to remember the view.

They say Mount Logan never rests,
chases Denali relentlessly. Tectonic
uplift, coupled with ice and snow
accumulation, temporarily increases
the growth rate from fingernail
to certain varieties of deciduous tree.

We imagine each other rising
along this line. Either one of us
could sleep at any moment.

VACATION'S WORTH

Five hundred eucalyptus trees line Maluhia Road
near Koloa Town. Planted in 1911, a gift
from a pineapple baron, they point the way
to his final resting place: eighth hole of a golf course
on the southern coast. Driving beneath them,
I can't see any evidence of two recent hurricanes.
Subtropical climate encourages instantaneous
regrowth, abundant foliage. Leaves form a feathered
ceiling over the road. I feel compelled to turn around
in my seat like Maria Schneider in *The Passenger*,
try to catch from this new angle, details
that may have passed undetected. There's a fear
in me: of watery depths, crusts of lava, headwinds
that threaten to blow us back where we came from.
At the blowhole near Poipu, molten rock layered
over sea water makes a spout for the ocean
to squirt through, a place to stare at when the sunset
is not quite enough. Above Mount Waialeale,
the wettest spot on earth, the sky clears its throat
between two torrential downpours. South of there,
past a deep, bean-shaped sand trap, a vacation's
worth of golf balls roll into the ocean.

Do you recognize me?

SUPERBOLIDE, CHELYABINSK

Fearing dry socket, I avoid straws after surgery. Keep my tongue clear of black holes, take capsules for pain. A star is erased from the chalkboard, another skims across the event horizon, peels off like a sticker in my hand. This one is special: gaining brightness, chewing space—it is not collapsing. Every few hours, I stop what I'm doing to repack the gauze in my cheek and the fear subsides. New report: superbolide in the Chelyabinsk region, east of the Ural Mountains. Bright flash followed by shock wave. Shattered windows in 3,600 apartment buildings. Twenty-five reported sunburns. Blame the painkillers, but I get it now: you can't fall through a hole inside yourself. If I could slingshot the meteor's flight path back through darkness, would I reach Jupiter's orbit as a human fireball and can a fireball be lonely? Overnight, a dozen blurry videos appear online. Dash cams on the icy continent tell the story flash blindness prevents, though they can't explain it: six-metre hole in Chebarkul Lake and everyone's impulse is to peer inside from the edge. Collective gasp as a half-ton chunk of four-billion-year-old rock is scooped from the bottom, hoisted back to the surface.

INFERNO

I.

As I turn my back to the lava lake, the bombs become imaginary.

Through ski goggles, I see objects scattered among paragraphs of snow.

Tent poles, thermal imager, broken camera, phonolite shards.

By night, my vision depletes.

I relocate to the crater's gritty opposite edge with a headlamp and a
   long tether.

Blurry as it is, the view is spectacular from any vantage.

I need medicine, clean drinking water.

I have altitude sickness and a sore toe.

From now on, I will try to take better care of myself.

To exercise, swallow vitamins, meditate daily.

As I track the bombs, the bombs are tracking me.

II.

After dinner, let's watch the documentary
about volcanoes. I want to see the exact
spot in Iceland where the livestock keeled over,
falling headfirst into the ground. Hydrofluoric
acid haze, sulphur dioxide headache, the poor
creatures contracted disease their tender
bones and teeth could not withstand. Then
New England saw the coldest, longest winters
on record, while ice floes bobbed like molars
in the Gulf of Mexico. We fall asleep
on the couch with only half an explanation
in our heads of how this happened. At 3 a.m.,
a slow slip event shakes BC's coast like a rattle
as I nurse our newborn son in the dark.
Consulting earthquaketrack.com with my free
hand only serves to point out the dozens
of recent tremors we hadn't noticed or felt.

A news report claims we're safe and tonight,
at least, I'll let that perspective win out.
Rank available information according
to shifting criteria I've just invented: We're safe!
It's a lie! We're safe! Renting this apartment
was a catastrophic mistake! This shopping centre
is designed to confuse visitors away from
the exits! This tropical bird sanctuary is a death
trap of triangular plate glass! Why are you
laughing? Sometimes I think we're on the same

page, and other times I worry that if someday
I flush our smartphones down the toilet,
you might not understand. But I'm certain we
can still find happiness in the world. We can
still retrieve our memories from a cloud.

III.

Dante approaches Erebus' lava lake as I sleep, heavy sheets pulled up around my head, arranged topographically.

I am so calm, this must be the future.

Land masses hold hands.

It's only a tiny bit dangerous.

Cross a slick little bridge of ice and *boom*, Antarctica!

Convenience nudges tourism up two-hundred percent MoM, YoY.

A gentle rustling sound beyond the tent flaps is incorporated into my dream.

Someone speaks into a microphone, mouth close to the wire mesh:

The high-tech aluminum spider will repel down vertical walls no human has ever touched with ease, sensors beeping, motors whirring like insects in flight, cameras recording each careful step.

Supportive penguins form a neat parade along the ice, stretching back 1.3 million years.

They feel the excitement, *Good luck, Dante!* spelled out in krill on the pack ice near McMurdo Sound.

Turns out, it's all talk.

On January 3, 1993, NASA pulls the plug when Dante's fibre-optic tether breaks, winter storms making a second attempt untenable.

When Mission Director Dave Lavery uses the phrase "unqualified success" to describe what didn't happen, I realize I am winning at life and dream no more.

Sheets the colour of ice and the sky are patient and always available to me. Glittering zippers to tamp down what floats up.

Before returning to his coffin of Styrofoam peanuts, Dante wistfully dips an aluminum toe into the crater, thinks of what might have been.

Bright applause is heard from within ice fumaroles dotting the volcanic landscape.

COMPOSITE: BLACK HOLE

I'm supermassive: a black hole
into which *billions of suns*
have disappeared. Interstellar
magnet, collapsed object, feature-
less by design. Folks at Hubble
speculate about my malevolence,
futz around with digital renderings.
Nestled deep inside elliptical galaxy
NGC 4889, *an egg-shaped swirl,*
I sulk and wait, knowing what I know.
Whipped meringue *monster*
in a porcelain mixing bowl.
For now, all is quiet in squid-ink
oblivion—I've lost my appetite
for stars. Full of secrets, pent-up
anxiety, I want someone to know me.

December 21, 2016:

New information,
incorrect instructions.

Jetliner misdirected in early morning,
flight path toward San Gabriel Mountains.

Mount Wilson rises above transmitters,

　　　　clear terrain.

Sound of television stations,
Southern Californians,
knocking,
　　　　signals.

Catastrophe relayed to officials,
　　　　　　too close to control.

SPACE MARBLE

*No Hazard (White): The likelihood of a collision is zero, or is so low
as to be effectively zero.*
– The Torino Scale

In her spare time, the astronaut
studies images from the Apollo spacecraft,
the ones that appeared in *Time*:
1972 blue marble with milk-white streams,
held in suspense by the click of the Hasselblad.
Zooming in, she recalls childhood games
in sepia salt trails, the playground microcosm,
shorthand of plainsies, clambroth.
Keeps zooming—her mind and the screen.
Swift blink sweeps her corneas clean.
What's the difference between zero
and effectively zero, anyway? There are
scenarios you can hold still, in a picture
or in your mind, and be consumed by them.
In all likelihood, this is not healthy.
In all likelihood, we are on a trajectory, unable
to stop. Not immortal after all.
For the tenth time in as many hours,
the astronaut erases clouds of breathdust
from the spaceship window, curses
the inherent loneliness of her situation.
Thinks: *If only I had never come here.*

Chemical light puddles, halogen fog.

Pool ice cracks in three places, snow smudges, dissolves.

*You put every earthly possession in a locker, pin the key to your
swimsuit strap.*

Tread water along the mildewed grid as leaves fall in.

You want to be pure displacement, the pride of Archimedes.

*You will not tamper with the touch pads, but you will shove ice blocks
aside with your elbows.*

*Look, there's Mount Baker, keeping watch over raspberry farms and
borderlands.*

*A mean smog, potent as antihistamine, obscures the peak when air
quality dips.*

*Wind nudges a skeletal tree branch into the water like one of those
drinking bird toys.*

Skiers telemark the Panorama Dome.

*With any luck, you'll soon be able to move your arms and legs like a
famous athlete.*

To butterfly-stroke slowly and evenly to the shallow end of the pool.

NEAR MISS

Meriting Attention by Astronomers (Yellow): A discovery, which
may become routine with expanded searches, of an object making
a somewhat close but not highly unusual pass near the Earth.
– The Torino Scale

1,056 close-Earth approaches since 1900.
Somewhat close, we're told, is not cause for alarm.
Yellow is neutral: beyond our control,
but not worrisome. I put fresh sheets on the bed
and wait. Today is February 4, 2011
and we are living our lives and not pretending.
At 19:39 UT, Asteroid 2011 CQ1 will make
a record pass, a mere 5,480 kilometres over
the mid-Pacific, closest non-impacting object to date.
I fold seven paper planes and wait. Snow film
on windows slides away with a *shhhh*. Robins
hold the delta up to their beaks and wait.
I feel funny today, can't feign anything. But I do
trust the scientists, their measurements
are a comfort. Tomorrow we might even be
grateful for near misses. On June 10, 2013,
a hot air balloon travelling from Scott County
State Fairgrounds to Prior Lake lands
on a highway near Chaska, Minnesota
without a single reported injury. Will it happen
again? I put a record under the needle and wait.
The sky is backlit and drooling particulate.
A car crashes on the corner, driver angling
for a better view. At this moment, someone is getting

a headache, someone is drafting a press release
and someone is tracking 1,397 potentially hazardous
asteroids from a modular workstation in Hawaii.

Threatening (Orange): A very close encounter by a large object,
which if occurring this century, poses an unprecedented but still
uncertain threat of a global catastrophe.
– The Torino Scale

At YVR, I do not zoom away from Earth. Code orange declared, I return to Gate C, segregated from the realm of speed and forward momentum. Walkie-talkies across the terminal crackle with synchronized static. A woman unfastens a snaking path of retractable belt stanchions, sweeps the area. I'm reading into this in ways I shouldn't, scanning the horizon for visual confirmation. There, dog kennels slide down conveyor belts they once hopefully ascended, followed by oversized sporting goods, collapsible strollers wrapped in plastic. If only I hadn't left you at the security checkpoint three hours prior to departure. If only we were still in the jungle, recording the staccato chirps of endangered Hawaiian birds, or something even sadder. I'd take sadness over soapy-looking clouds and uncertainty. It's fine. I just need to know if circumstances have gotten to the point where I could run backwards through the beeping scanners to find you and that wouldn't be perceived as crazy. Guess I'll wait until my checked baggage floats back to me or I see fire raining on the animals. Until then, sit quietly on this blue vinyl bench where no one else is sitting. Taxiway lights stop blinking, shifting my gaze to the window's outer edges: a pedestrian walkway. Hanging from the terminal like a starched shirt sleeve, it sits beneath an encroaching shadow of vague dimension. Looks viable right up until the moment it disappears.

Do you know where you are?

EMERGENCY PREPAREDNESS

Certain Collisions (Red): A collision is certain, capable of causing global climatic catastrophe that may threaten the future of civilization as we know it, whether impacting land or ocean. Such events occur on average once per 100,000 years, or less often.
– The Torino Scale

As the planet rose to an unfamiliar new temperature, I recalled a night course in emergency preparedness, something about how low elevations never fare well. Repositioning the telescope to a higher vantage point, we spied a mountain dense with evergreens, and there, a few remaining amenities: reputable cat hospital, small orchard of pippins. We struggled with the proportions of it, seriously considered going before deciding not to. With a nod of resignation, you threw a tarp over the bicycles, lawnmower, croquet set, still allowing for a little hopefulness amid our overwhelming uncertainty about the future. The last time we looked outside the air was woolly with ash and the tarp was disappearing. Or was it? Did we go to the attic, tilt a favourite album against the light to check for scratches? Did music hide your footfalls across the floor? Maybe we never made it up the stairs, but I like to think we held each other and listened to songs, thankful for that dim, private space behind the eyelids that was not the world.

COMPOSITE: OUT OF ORBIT

I'm kung fu. Algae.
A canoe filled with rain.
Storm clouds, Cartesian coordinates.
Disaster response route
and runaway lane. Ivied Ferris
wheel in Pripyat. Enrichment
course in the Rocky Mountains.
Photocopier, scotch tape dispenser.
I'm White-Out. A woven lawn
chair. Past participle,
completed action. Out of orbit.
Disproportional. Disinherited.
A dress rehearsal, a first draft.
Midnight dispatch. Water-soluble.
Gloomy. Insufferable. I quiver
like Jell-O, drain like a kiddie pool.
I'm leftovers. Foliage and groundcover.
An airlock, a dying star.

AFTER THE COMET...

... I didn't remember a mountain
                        being in that location,
            swore I'd never

                seen it before. Believed
the acupuncture needles quivering on your toes
            were tiny weathervanes

                or antennae

                        beaming radio signals
into space.

That your sleep cycles

                and my leg pain

                had dramatically improved in recent weeks.

In the face of naysayers,
we held
nothing back. A pure belief

                persisted between us—

like a Mylar blanket or charcoal filter,
            it was protection enough.

Surface, interior,
liquid, gas,

rock:

    night air swirling with microscopic particles.

    Adrift in this landscape,
        we held artificial light up to ancient ghosts,

       then exhaled them.

Between glass slides, they changed again.

Maybe you're right:
it's been so long now,
who's to say what really happened.

But in the years since,

    we've scarcely trespassed a receiving line

      or uttered a   *How are your parents?*

Now, we almost always send regrets.

TWIN ATMOSPHERES

I was inside the volcano.

I was standing at the edge.

I was standing back from the edge, zooming in with my phone.

I was asking strangers to take my camera closer than I was willing to go.

I was watching the eruption on the six o'clock news.

I was re-watching the eruption on YouTube, from different angles.

I was watching shaky, hand-held videos of the eruption.

I was watching videos shot from the window of a helicopter.

I was watching lava devour moss, rock, kite strings.

I saw the interstate become lava.

I saw supervisors and analysts standing up and pointing.

I knew what a volcano calls itself in private.

My heart was a darkened cinema in which the aisles are rivers of lava.

I had a low-grade fever.

I stopped dreaming.

I lost the ability to blend in.

I inhabited twin atmospheres.

I inhabited geological time. I patterned new systems.

I demonstrated evacuation procedures.

I knew where all the dead ends were.

I was waiting for the eruption to begin again.

I was waiting for lava to turn from liquid red to solid black.

I was waiting for the formation of block lava.

I was waiting for pāhoehoe.

I was waiting for valleys and mountains and domes.

I was waiting for tubes, lakes and fountains.

USED TO

*Normal (Green): Current calculations show the chance of collision is
extremely unlikely with no cause for public attention or public concern.*
– The Torino Scale

Men used to have names like Buck,
Lawrence, take the tour at Cape Canaveral
with their wives and children. Everyone smoked
inside the Launch Control Center.
We used to build replicas with toothpicks,
wood glue, recite the go/no go poll.
Strapped to homemade rockets, our wishes
passed the status check. Rich kids
used to go to college, but enrolment is low
this semester. Some demand refunds,
though the opt-out deadline was two weeks ago.
We used to lie on hoods of sport utility vehicles,
wait for icy LINEAR to pass. While most comets
appeared to be backing out of the universe,
this one trailed bright daughter fragments
of dust and ice beyond the Kármán line.
I worried a little, extending my arms upward
as if to push the glittering thing back
into darkness. Seventy-four million miles
feels closer at night. At night we used to go
to North Dakota. Without documentation,
we'd swing backpacks, dreams over the ditch.
I used to hold my breath until they landed.

Close calls,
safety improvements.
Data is safe,
could be safer.

Intersections of safety,
one thought until it happens.

"I think about it a little,"

plane,
truck,
ranked collision.

Wrap up,
stop.

Guide the passengers near Orlando.

DRAWBRIDGE [*Dream*]

Car hangs by a thread from the bascule leaf,

emergency brake clenching metal,

momentary stillness.

Not much we can do at this point,

ninety degrees to the bridge deck,

our hair falling like a curtain into the back seat,

cassettes from the dash split open on the rear window.

Next stop: the territory of rockets or swimmers?

Your eyes are telling me we should get used to this feeling,

leaning away from the earth

as the earth comes up to meet us.

NOTES

The Joy Division epigraph is a lyric from their song "Transmission," released in 1979.

The dates cited in the opening dream poem correspond to the five largest known earthquakes to occur in British Columbia, according to a 2014 news report from the CBC.

"Decommissioned Planes" was inspired in part by a description of the Mojave Boneyard from the website: lostamerica.com.

"[*Testimony*]" is an erasure poem based on the article "FAA records detail hundreds of close calls between airplanes and drones," by Craig Whitlock published in *The Washington Post* on August 20, 2015. The line in quotations is a direct quote from Chuck Schumer.

The quoted phrase in "Proximity Sensors" is taken from the Wikipedia entry of the same name.

The quoted lines in "Cartography" are from the map entitled "Energy Resources of British Columbia, 1982" published by Canadian Cartographics Ltd.

"Interior Mysteries" was inspired in part by a story in *The Daily Mail* entitled "Dropping £45,000 piano 'was the worst thing that's ever happened to me.'"

"[*Testimony: Westchester*]" is an erasure poem based on the online news report, "Investigators Exclusive: Close call as planes nearly collide over Westchester," by Jim Hoffer from ABC *Eyewitness News*, which aired Friday, January 30, 2015.

"After Your Funeral" was inspired in part by *My Architect: A Son's Journey*, the 2003 documentary film about American architect Louis Kahn.

"[*Testimony: JFK*]" is an erasure poem based on the online news report, "FAA investigating after Delta pilot reports close call with drone before landing at JFK airport," by Josh Einiger from ABC *Eyewitness News*, which aired Saturday, August 1, 2015.

The italicized lines in "Inferno" are a quote from a *New York Times* article by Warren E. Leary entitled "Robot Named Dante To Explore Inferno of Antarctic Volcano," published December 8, 1992. "Inferno" also makes reference to the 2016 Werner Herzog documentary film, *Into the Inferno*.

The italicized words in "Composite: Black Hole" are quotes from a *New York Times* article by Dennis Overbye entitled "Astronomers Find Biggest Black Holes Yet," published December 5, 2011.

"Testimony: Mount Wilson" is an erasure poem based on the online news report, "New data show misdirected jet's close call with Mount Wilson," by Rob Hayes from ABC *Eyewitness News*, which aired Wednesday, December 21, 2016.

The Torino Scale epigraphs were taken directly from the NASA website.

The statistics cited in "Near Miss" are also from the NASA website.

"[*Testimony: Orlando*]" is an erasure poem based on the online news report, "FAA investigates close calls at Orlando Sanford International Airport," by Field Sutton from *WFTV TV Ch 9* (ABC), Orlando (FL), which aired Wednesday, March 22, 2017.

ACKNOWLEDGEMENTS

These poems were written between 2013–2017. I am grateful to the editors of the journals in which they first appeared, some in different forms: *Arc Poetry Magazine*, *The Burnside Review* (US), *Contemporary Verse 2*, *The Dalhousie Review*, EVENT, *The Fiddlehead*, PRISM international, *Queen's Quarterly*, *Qwerty*, *Riddle Fence*, *Sidereal Magazine* (US), *Vallum* and *The Best Canadian Poetry in English 2013*.

Thank you to the Writers' Trust of Canada for generously supporting my work in progress and publishing several of these poems as an e-book for the 2013 RBC Bronwen Wallace Award for Emerging Writers.

Thank you to Amber McMillan for thoughtful, incisive edits, Carleton Wilson for the brilliant cover design and to Silas White and everyone at Nightwood Editions for making this real.

Thank you to Ryan Peter for the perfect, volcanic cover art.

Thank you to the Writer's Studio at Simon Fraser University and Jen Currin for getting me started on this path and inspiring confidence in me.

Thank you to The Banff Centre for the Arts, where I wrote some of these poems during a six-week residency in 2013, and especially to Karen Solie for thoughtful discussions and encouragement during that time.

My eternal gratitude to Sheryda Warrener, the best, most generous reader any poet could ask for.

Warm thanks to the steadfast and wonderful Lindsay Cuff, Dina Del Bucchia, Senka Kovacevic, Clayton Misura, Kellee Ngan, Kim Nguyen and Tara Sawatsky.

Thank you to my family.

All my love to Benjamin and Jonathan—for as long as it lasts, I am lucky to share this life on this planet with you.

ABOUT THE AUTHOR

Laura Matwichuk's poems have appeared in literary journals in Canada, the US and in *The Best Canadian Poetry in English*. She was a finalist for the RBC Bronwen Wallace Award for Emerging Writers and shortlisted for *Arc Poetry* Magazine's Poem of the Year. Matwichuk lives in Vancouver, BC.

PHOTO CREDIT: JONATHAN BITZE